Francis Fry, Miles Coverdale

The Bible by Coverdale, MDXXXV

Francis Fry, Miles Coverdale

The Bible by Coverdale, MDXXXV

ISBN/EAN: 9783337099848

Printed in Europe, USA, Canada, Australia, Japan

Cover: Foto ©Lupo / pixelio.de

More available books at **www.hansebooks.com**

THE
Bible by Coverdale

MDXXXV.

REMARKS ON THE TITLES; THE YEAR OF PUBLICATION;
THE PRELIMINARY; THE WATER-MARKS, &c.

WITH FAC-SIMILES.

BY

FRANCIS FRY, F.S.A.

MYLES COVERDALE.

LONDON: WILLIS & SOTHERAN. BRISTOL: LASBURY.

1867.

CONTENTS.

A2

CONTENTS OF THE PLATES.

N.B.—This book consists of 15 Plates Fac-similes, No. 1 to 15; Title and three leaves, signature A, pp. i. to viii.; signatures B to F 2, pp. 1 to 10.

COLLATION

OF THE FIRST BIBLE IN ENGLISH.

Eight leaves before the text printed in English black-letter.

1.—The Title.—Reverse: blank. Date 1535. [Plate 2.] The letter-press is surrounded with wood-cuts of subjects from the Scriptures, and Henry VIII. under a canopy with attendants and Royal Arms, and six quotations from the Bible.

2. ✠ ii.—"Unto the most victorious Prynce." [Plate 5.]

3. ✠ iii.—Dedication, continued.

4. ✠ iiii.—Dedication, concluded. [Plate 8, No. 7.]

Rev.: "A prologe Myles Couerdale Unto the Christen reader."

5. ✠ v.—To the reader, continued.

6.—To the reader, continued.

7.—To the reader, concluded.

Reverse: "The bokes of the hole Byble" as far as Malachy.

8.—The List of the books, concluded.—Reverse: "The first boke of Moses/ called Genesis, what this boke conteyneth."

There is a title dated 1535, [Plate 1] and one leaf of pre-liminary, [Pl. 6, No. 5] printed in the same type as the Bible.

There is a title, dated 1536, printed in English bl.-let. [Pl. 3.]

The contents of the chapters are placed before each book, except that none are given to "Salomons Balettes," "The Laments' of Jeremy," "The songe of the iij. children," "The story of Susanna," and "The story of Bel," and that the contents are placed before each chapter of Hester in the Apocrypha.

The Bible begins, "The first boke of Moses, called Genesis." [Pl. 14, No. 1.] Fol. 1, signature a. Half this page is occupied with wood-cuts of the six "dayes worke." The first chapter commences with a capital I fourteen lines deep. [Pl. 14, No. 2.]

Deuteronomy ends on the recto, folio 90, p 6.—The reverse: blank. Then follows a map the size of two leaves—no doubt a wood-cut—it measures to the outside line, $15\frac{3}{4}$ inches by $11\frac{3}{4}$. Above the map is printed "The descripcion of the londe of promes called Palestina/ Canaan or the holy londe." The map is drawn with the north to the bottom and the south to the top.

A title: "The seconde parte of the olde Testament," with a list of books, Joshua to Hester.—On the reverse of the title, the contents of Joshua. Joshua begins folio 2, aa ij. Part 2 ends on the reverse of folio 120, vv 6.

Job begins folio I, Aa. There is no title here as in other parts where the folios and a signature commence again. Job, the Psalms, &c., end folio 52, J i 4.—Reverse: blank.

A title: "All the Prophetes in Englishe," with a list of books, Esay to Malachy.—On the reverse: the contents of Esay. Esay begins folio 2, Aaa ij, and Malachy ends on the reverse of folio 102, Rrr. 6.

A title: "Apocripha," and list of books, Esdras to Maccabees. —On the reverse: The translator to the reader and the contents of Esdras. The 3rd book of Esdras begins folio 2, A ij. The 2nd Maccabees ends on the reverse of folio 83, for 81, O 5.

A title: "The new testament," with a list of books, Matthew to The Revelation.—On the rev. the contents of Matthew. Matthew begins folio 2, AA ij. The Revelation ends on the rev. folio 113, TT 5. The Imprint is on this page. [Plate 14, No. 4.]

The letter-press of the last four titles is surrounded with wood-cuts, Scriptural and ornamental.

I have seen variations in six leaves :—folio 67, 4th book of Moses, in some copies the signature is m, in one copy, M.—In five leaves these misprints: 2nd Esdras, folio 113, in error 112 —Esay, folio 5, in error 2—Jeremiah, folio 46, in error 45— 2nd Corinthians, folio 81, in error 71—Lamentations, folio 49, ta repeated. Probably these errors were corrected in the progress of printing, and not an evidence of another edition, as has been supposed. See Herbert, p. 1545.

There are many wood-cuts placed in the text. [See Pl. 15.]

A full page contains 57 lines.

WHEN we consider Coverdale's character in all its different bearings, and, above all, his labours in presenting to the inhabitants of this country, and all the nations of the world who speak the English language, the scriptures in their native tongue; the name of Coverdale is one which will be always mentioned with veneration and respect.

Remains of Myles Coverdale, Parker Society, p. xix.

THE BIBLE BY COVERDALE.

HE BIBLE FIRST PRINTED in the English language is known as the Version by Myles Coverdale, because the "Epistle unto the Kynges hyghnesse." bears his name at the conclusion of it, thus,—"youre graces humble subiecte and daylye oratour, Myles Couerdale." [See Plate 8, No. 7.] The laborious work of translating and printing the Bible was completed in the reign of Henry the Eighth.

There are many circumstances relating to the production of this interesting book of which we should like to have been informed: but after much research the information that has reached us is exceedingly scanty.

We know when the Volume was printed. It concludes with the Imprint, which is on the reverse of

B

the last leaf, thus,—"Prynted in the yeare of oure
LORDE M.D.XXXV. and fynished the fourth daye
of October."

As to the Translator, perhaps no more is known
than Coverdale himself has communicated to us.
In the Dedication he says—"Considerynge now
(most gracyous prynce) the inestimable treasure,
frute & prosperite euerlastynge, that God geueth
with his worde, and trustynge in his infynite goodnes that he woulde brynge my symple and rude
laboure herin to good effecte, therfore as the holy
goost moued other men to do the cost herof, so was
I boldened in God, to laboure in the same."

"I thought it my dutye and to belonge vnto my
allegiaunce, whan I had translated this Bible, not
onely to dedicate this translacyon vnto youre hyghnesse, but wholy to commytte it vnto the same."
"And as I do with all humblenes submitte myne
vnderstondynge and my poore translacyon vnto the
spirite of trueth in your grace, so make I this pro-
testacyon (hauyng God to recorde in my conscience)
that I haue nether wrested nor altered so moch as
one worde for the mayntenaunce of any maner of
secte : but haue with a cleare conscience purely &
faythfully translated this out of fyue sundry interpreters, hauyng onely the manyfest trueth of the

scripture before myne eyes." In his Prologue to the reader he says, "Consiberynge" "how weake I am to perfourme the office of translatoure, I was the more lothe to medle with this worke." Further on he says, "(acordyng as I was desyred) I toke the more vpon me to set forth this speciall translacyon." In several places he alludes to the work as his own, thus,—"And this maner haue I vsed in my translacyon, callyng it in some place pennaunce, that in another place I call repentaunce." We have no information that he was assisted by any scholars of the day, whilst from the passages quoted it is clear that Coverdale intended that he should be regarded as the sole translator.

We do not know when Coverdale began the work of translating. In the Dedication to King Edward the Sixth, in the quarto edition, 1550, he says, "therfore was I boldened in God sixtene yeares agoo, not only to laboure faythfully in the same, but also in most humble wyse to dedicate this my pore translation to your graces moost noble father." In the Prologue to the same edition, we read, "(accordinge as I was desyred. Anno, 1.5.34.) I toke the more vpon me, to set forth this specyall translacion." These passages do not I think imply that he began the work of translating in the year

B2

1534, although it has been argued from this statement that Coverdale translated and printed the
Bible in eleven months. Can it mean more than
that he commenced the printing necessary to the
publication of it? Indeed it would have been im-
possible to have achieved so gigantic a work in the
time mentioned. The Editor of the "Remains of
Myles Coverdale," published by the Parker Society,
p. ix., says, "It is probable that Coverdale was
labouring by himself in retirement," "as we lose
sight of him almost entirely after the year 1528
till 1535, when he published, on the fourth of
October, his translation of the whole Bible; a work,
on which it is probable that he had been employed
for some years, although we have no evidence at
what time he commenced it."

We have not been informed where Coverdale re-
sided whilst he was engaged in the work of translation.
The title and some preliminary matter were printed
in the same type as the Bible and also in the English
black letter, but why these were twice printed, or by
whom, we do not know; nor has any Bibliographer
yet been able to inform us with what title-page this
most interesting book was first issued in this country.

It yet remains a mystery from what Press it was
issued.

It is with the intention of clearing up the difficulty that has been felt relating to the titles, that I commence these Remarks, feeling sure that any information in addition to that already recorded, cannot be devoid of interest to all conversant with this branch of bibliography, and especially to those who are possessors of the First Bible in English. I propose also, to allude to a few questions which have been raised by some authors who have written on this subject.

The text is preceded by one gathering of eight leaves, of which the second, third, fourth, and fifth only have the signature, as copied, Plate 6. These eight leaves contain the Title,—the Dedication to King Henry the Eighth and "with your dearest and iust wyfe, and most vertuous Pryncesse, Quene Anne."—"A prologue. Myles Couerdale Unto the Christen reader."—"The bokes of the hole Byble," —and "The first boke of Moses/ called Genesis what this boke conteyneth." All copies or parts of this preliminary matter known to exist, with the exception of two copies of one title and one leaf, which will be described, are printed in black-letter type such as was used in England at this time. This is so far plain, but it has been difficult to decide with what title the Bible was published. Four copies of the title-page have been known, two of which have the date 1535, and the other two that of 1536. One of those of 1535 is in the Bible belonging to the Earl of Leicester, Holkham Hall—the other is in the Library of the British Museum, but not quite perfect. These titles read thus,—" Biblia The Bible/ that is, the holy Scripture of the Olde and New Testament, faithfully and truly translated out of Douche and Latyn in to Englishe. M.D.XXXV." [See Plate 1.] The letter-press of the title, with the list of the Books as far as Malachi, on the reverse, is from the same type as that with which the text is printed. One of the titles of 1536 is in the Bible belonging to the Earl of Jersey, and the other is in the Bible in the Library of Gloucester Cathedral. The letter-press of the titles of 1536 is English black-letter, and reads thus,—" Biblia The Byble : that is/ the holy Scrypture of the Olde and New Testament, faythfully translated in to Englyshe. M.D.XXXVI." [See Plate 3.] Dibden, in his "Spenceriana," vol. 1, p. 81, says, "The Earl of Northampton has a perfect copy:" but he does not allude to the title.

If the title of 1535, as described, is placed in a Bible with the Dedication, &c., printed in English black-letter, it is obvious that the first part of the

List of the Books occurs twice, namely, on the back of the title and on the reverse of the seventh leaf; but it cannot be supposed that the Volume was so issued, with the contents of one page in duplicate. Anderson, in his "Annals of The English Bible," (vol. I. p. 562.) gives "the Title and Collation" of the first Bible, and describes the title, [Plate 1.] omitting the List of the Books which is on the reverse of it; perhaps because he did not know how to account for such an error as the contents of a page repeated in the same volume. To avoid this error of a duplicate List of the Books, the title of 1536, which is blank on the reverse, has been considered by some writers to be the title with which the Bible was first issued, and because the letter-press is from the same type as the preliminary leaves one of which contains the List of the Books. But by receiving this title as the one which was issued in the Bible on its publication, a new difficulty arises. Why was the publication postponed, from the time when the printing was finished, October the fourth, 1535, to 1536, the date on the title in English type; which, if not issued until after the death of Queen Anne, was about eight months?

Lewis, in his History, is the first writer, as far as I have been able to trace, who has endeavoured to explain this supposed delay of the publication. He describes Coverdale's Bible with the Dedication to the King and Queen Jane, and then the Imprint, the fourth of October, 1535; and adds, "This is a plain inconsistency with the Title or Preamble of the Dedication," "wherein, as has been before observed, *Coverdale* mentions the King's *dearest just wife* JANE, whereas it is certain, that the King was not married to Her till *May*, 20, 1536. more than half a Year after the Date of finishing this Bible. The only way I can think of to reconcile this Difference, is this; That, after this Bible's being finished at the Press in *October*, *Coverdale*, hearing from his Friends in *England*, that Queen *Anne* was declining at Court, thought it prudent to defer the Publication of it till he saw what Turn Affairs would take, and after the King's marrying Queen *Jane*, who was thought to favor the Reformation, then made the fore-mentioned Dedication to the King, or however altered the Title of it as it stands now, and reprinted it." (Lewis' History, folio, 1731, p. 25.) This suggestion has been adopted by subsequent writers and become current as if it was an established fact.

I may here also notice the opinions of Professor Walter and Chr. Anderson, who adopt the same mode of accounting for the supposed delay.

Professor Walter in his Letter says, "Coverdale's Bible, though not published till 1536, bears the date of 1535." "The interval between the date on the title-page and the actual publication is clearly marked by a curious alteration in the dedicatory letter to Henry VIII. which contains these words, "your dearest just wife, and most vertuous pryncesse Qu. JAne." This is not as it was printed; for Anne has been altered into JAne by the pen."* Professor Walter must have supposed that the alteration was so made, generally in the edition, as one copy altered with the pen would not be sufficient ground on which to argue that the name had been changed by the direction of Coverdale himself, which is what appears to be intended by the remark.

Anderson adopts the opinion of Professor Walter, and at considerable length endeavours to show that this Bible was not published till 1536. He says, "The death of Queen Anne in May 1536, having proved fatal to the appearance of this book till after the event, various expedients were then tried to ensure success." The passage already given from Walter's Letter is then quoted, and Anderson goes

* "A Letter to the Rt. Rev. Herbert, Lord Bishop of Peterborough," "on the Independence of the Authorized Version of the Bible. By Henry Walter, B.D. and F.R.S.," &c. London. 1823. 8vo., p. 72.

C

on to say that the British Museum copy has Anne
altered to Jane with the pen, "Lambeth Library
has one copy with Anne, another with Jane. The
Bodleian has Anne. Sion College has Jane, and
in some copies the *name* of the Queen had been
expunged." "Only one other device remained to be
tried, which was that of a new title, as if it were
a different book; changing the year to the next,
or 1536, and leaving out the words "translated *out
of Douch and Latyn.*" " (Annals, vol. 1, p. 563.)

The late Mr. Botfield held the same opinion.
Describing the Bibles by Coverdale in Lambeth
Library, he says, "The second of these copies, has
the dedication to Queen Jane Seymour, belonging
to the edition 1536," (Cathedral Libraries, p. 193.)
There does not appear to be any authority for the
supposition that this leaf with "Queen Jane" was
printed for the edition of 1536; the evidence is
quite the other way, for neither of the only two
copies with the title of 1536 have the "Jane" leaf,
but they have the Dedication with "Queen Anne."

All these arguments have arisen from an error.
Had those authors examined the "Queen Jane"
leaf of Dedication they would have found that it is
none other than a leaf of Nycolson's Coverdale of
1537, which had been inserted to complete the copy.

I have fac-similes of all the preliminary leaves of
this Bible of 1537; and, in order to be very sure, I
have compared the first leaf of the Dedication with
the original in the Baptist College, Bristol, and
placed line against line, and most carefully examined
every letter. The fac-simile being correct, in the
same way I compared it with the "Jane" leaf in
Sion College, and I can say that the Sion College
leaf is identical with Nycolson's leaf of 1537. On
the second page of this edition, t is omitted from
traytoure, being printed "trayoure;" [See a copy,
Plate 8, No. 3.] it is the same in the Sion College
leaf: such an error is not likely to have occurred in
two editions. That this "Jane" leaf is one of Nycolson's edition is confirmed by the fact that the four
following leaves in the volume are from Nycolson's
Bible. The second leaf of Nycolson's Dedication
has, in line thirty, "CHRIT" for CHRIST; this
error is in the leaf following the "Jane" leaf in
the Sion College Bible of 1535. I have also examined all the "Jane" leaves named by Anderson,
and those also are of the edition of 1537. The
head-lines of the Dedication and Prologue in the
Bible of 1535, are in very different type from
those in Nycolson's Bible, 1537. Compare Plate
6, No. 1, 2, 3, 4. and Plate 8, No. 1, 2, 4, 5.

C2

The signatures differ—compare those on Plates 6 and 8.

The first Bible has been always designated as a book of 1535, but if the title of 1536 was that with which it was issued, it should be placed under 1536—and I believe no bibliographer has ever so arranged it. And further to show that this Bible has been generally admitted to be of the year 1535, copies have been usually completed with a fac-simile of the title of 1535 like the text, though followed by the seven leaves printed in the English type,—thus making the anomaly of the List of the Books in duplicate.

The difficulties which have been described, at once vanish when we learn that there is in existence a title with the date 1535, printed in the English black-letter. It has, I believe, never been described. The Marquis of Northampton has a very fine copy with this title. The volume is perfect, with the exception of the Map. The title is printed from wood blocks, no doubt the same as those used for the other title of 1535, and for that of 1536. The letter-press is from the English type, and the year 1535 is plainly printed. It reads—"Biblia The Byble : that is/ the holy Scrypture of the Olde and New Testament, faythfully translated in to

Englyshe. M.D.XXXV." [See Plate 2.] It will
be observed that there is an important difference
between the two titles of 1535; the one now described does not contain these words "translated out
of Douche and Latyn" which occur on the other
title. If the preliminary leaves and the title as part
of it in the type of the text, were not issued in this
country with the Bible,—and the evidence seems to
show that they were not,—may we not fairly conclude that Myles Coverdale did not wish to publish
such a statement on the title as the character of
his version. We know also, that these words were
omitted from the title of 1536, from the editions
by Nycolson, 1537, in folio and quarto, and from
all subsequent editions.

There is a great mistake in the title of the quarto
edition of Coverdale's Bible, 1550, printed by Froschover, with his name and his device of the tree
and frogs, which is preserved in the Library at
Zurich. It reads thus, "truly and purely transslated
into Englische/ by Mayst. Thomas Mathewe." We
cannot suppose that Coverdale himself, or any one
on his behalf, could have originated so great an error
as to call his version by the name given to that by
Tyndale and Rogers of 1537. There is also this
error in the title of the New Testament printed by

Froschover, 1550. It reads—"translated by Miles
Couerdal." whereas it is Tyndale's Version. As we
know these errors have been made, it is quite possible that the printer of the Bible of 1535 may have
inserted words which the great translator would not
adopt: and the introduction of the words "out of
Douche and Latyn" may have been one reason why
the title with these words was suppressed, whether
placed there by Coverdale himself, or by some one
else. This view is confirmed by his own statement
in the Dedication to the King, where he says he has
"with a cleare conscience purely & faythfully translated this out of fyue sundry interpreters, hauying
onely the manyfest trueth of the scripture before
myne eyes."

In the Letter to Lord Cromwell,—dated Paris,
June 23, 1538,—by Coverdale and Grafton, is this
passage, "For we follow not only a standing text
of the Hebrew, with the interpretation of the
Chaldee and the Greek; but we set also in a private
table the diversity of readings of all texts, with
such annotations in another table, as shall doubt-
less elucidate and clear the same." [Remains, p.
492.] Although this was written when Coverdale
was engaged in revising the "Great Bible" of 1539,
yet we may fairly conclude he used the books to

which he alludes when he was translating the Bible of 1535.

J. W. Whittaker, M.A., has gone very fully into the merits of Coverdale's Version as an original translation. He shows, by an examination of many passages, that Coverdale did translate from the Hebrew, although he used the five interpreters to help him. He says, if " this statement" (translated out of Dutch and Latin,) "is taken out of the title-page, which I can neither deny nor confirm, not having been able to consult a copy in which it is preserved," " the title-page contains a very great misrepresentation."*

The next passage I shall quote is from Todd's Life of Bishop Walton, (p. 98.) " At the head of those in the reign of Henry VIII, who have benefitted their country by their skill in languages, must ever stand the names of Tyndale and Coverdale; men, who eminently proved themselves by their knowledge of learning, meet for the people " "in presenting them with Versions of the Sacred Text from the original tongues ; men to whom the sound scholar still appeals with admiration."

---

* The Interpretation of the Hebrew Scriptures, &c. J. W. Whittaker, M.A., 1819, p. 59.

Anderson (vol. 1, p. 564) reviewing this subject,
considers that " With reference, however, to the
Bible brought into England in 1536, of Coverdale's
qualifications as a Translator from the original, there
can be little or rather no question," and concludes
that the words "translated out of Douche and
Latyn" were withdrawn by Coverdale himself in
1536.

The author of the Biographical Notice of Myles
Coverdale (The Remains, p. xvii) comes to the same
conclusion. He says it is not consistent with his
object " to enter into an elaborate discussion of the
merits of Coverdale as a translator; yet it may be
permitted to remark, that although he professes to
have consulted both the Latin and German transla-
tions, his version throughout bears marks of a close
attention to the original."

I am aware that some writers have taken a different view of the question, but my object is not to
prove that Coverdale translated from the Hebrew,
but only to show that it is probable the title-page
in the same type as the text, was not intended by
Coverdale himself to have been prefixed to any
copies of the Bible of his translation.

The Title, the Dedication, and the other leaves
before the text in the Marquis of Northampton's

copy are printed from the English type, and are the
same as those in other copies of this Bible. The
first eight leaves are in the same type, and the date
on the title and on the last leaf of the Bible agree.
The reverse of the title is blank, and the first part
of the List of the Books is on the reverse of the
seventh leaf. Lord Compton very courteously informed me that this title was in the Library at Castle
Ashby, and through his Lordship's introduction I
have been allowed to have a copy taken and to
describe the title.

In the Bible of 1535 belonging to the Earl of
Leicester, at Holkham Hall, having the title before
described, is one leaf printed in the same type as
the title and as the volume itself. It is the only
one known to exist printed in this type, and is most
interesting as proving that some introductory matter
was printed in the same type as the work; it also
affords strong evidence that the title with the List
of Books on the reverse of it, was not intended to
accompany the Dedication, &c., which was printed
in the English black-letter. This leaf has on the
recto the conclusion of the Prologue to the reader,
of which there is more on this page than there is on
the corresponding page of the Prologue in English
black-letter. The first line begins "are able to

D

make satisfaction unto God." [See Plate 6, No. 5.] It reads the same as the other Prologue, except that "God of his mercy preserue all his," in the English black-letter Prologue reads, "god of his mercy and plenteous goodnes preserue all his." and that on the reverse of this leaf there is " &c." after " Chap. vi " more than there is in the contents of Genesis in the other leaf. On the reverse of the Earl of Leicester's leaf we find " The first boke of Moses, called Genesis. What this boke conteyneth." Corresponding to this, that is on the reverse of the last page of the Prologue in the usual preliminary matter, is the page "The bokes of the hole Byble," while the last part of the List of the Books and the contents of Genesis, fill the next or eighth leaf.

It is very satisfactory that this particular leaf has been preserved, because it shews a different arrangement of the introductory matter: we may conclude from it that the first part of the List of the Books which formed part of the preliminary matter in the same type as the Bible, was printed only on the reverse of the title. The List of the Books being printed on the reverse of the seventh leaf of the English printed preliminary leaves, proves that it was intended to follow a Title without a List of the Books on the reverse. Through the courtesy of

the Earl of Leicester I was permitted to examine the
leaf which I have described, and to have a tracing
taken of it. As to the leaves which followed the
title in the Earl of Leicester's Bible we know not
why they were disused. We know only what the
one leaf now remaining shows us; as it does not
contain the beginning of the Prologue to the Reader
there must have been more than one leaf of preliminary, but how many we do not know. Although the
title and the preliminary leaves in the type of the
text, may have been set aside for the reasons
suggested, there may have been other motives for
the course which was adopted, of which we are
ignorant. If the lost leaves should be discovered
it will be seen wherein they differ from those that
were probably printed by Nycolson. Let the facts
which are brought forward have their due weight,
be the conclusions from them what they may.

By a happy coincidence I am able to describe at
the same time, the title belonging to the Marquis
of Northampton, and the leaf in the Earl of Leicester's copy of the Bible, as the evidence afforded
by each clearly points to the same conclusion.

As all copies, except the Earl of Leicester's,
which have any original leaves before the text, have
those which are supposed to have been printed in

re

England, it now appears certain that such as are completed with a fac-simile title should have one the same as that in the Bible belonging to the Marquis of Northampton, if it is intended that the copy should represent the Bible as it was first sent out by Myles Coverdale. It also follows that all copies which have fac-similes of the title the same as the text inserted, are incorrect, and do not represent any edition of the Bible.

The English black-letter titles of 1535 and 1536 differ from the other title by two lines. Those in the woodcuts below A and B, Plate 1, are not found in either of the other titles, nor in that by Nycolson, 1537. [See Plates 2, 3, and 4.] The type of the usual preliminary matter and that of the Northampton title and the two of 1536 appear to be the same as that used for the introductory matter of the folio edition of 1537; some of the pages of which read with it line for line. Can there be any doubt, therefore, that James Nycolson, of Southwark, printed these two titles and the following leaves? Compare fac-similes on Plates 5 and 6 with those on Plates 7 and 8.

The error which Lewis, Professor Walter, and others have made in supposing that the first leaf of the Dedication was reprinted for the editions of

1535 or 1536, shows how neccessary it is for bibliographers to know that the copy of the work on
which they write is a correct example of the edition.
This is particularly important when describing early
editions of the Bible, which are often found made up
of two or more editions. When we remember the
persecution the Sacred Volume had to endure, as
well as the injury to which it was subjected from
frequent use, it may easily be conceived that many
copies became imperfect, and needed repair at no
very distant period from the time of publication:
and, therefore, that missing leaves were occasionally
supplied from any edition which would answer the
purpose. Many Bibles and New Testaments were
no doubt so made up at an early period, whilst
others were first issued composed of two or more
editions which would read together. Thus, portions
of the three editions of Tyndale's New Testament
in quarto, 1536, are sometimes found in the same
volume. So, likewise, the two editions of the New
Testament in quarto, printed by Nycolson, 1538.
The Great Bible, 1539, and the six editions of
Cranmer's Version, and also the Large Folios of
the Authorised Version, are much mixed, which is
proved in a work lately published.* I have seen

* "A DESCRIPTION OF THE GREAT BIBLE. 1539, AND THE

the last leaf of Cranmer's Version, by Whitchurch,
1553, in the edition of 1549, with which that leaf
will read; and in a copy of Matthew's Version,
1537, the List of the Books of the edition by

SIX EDITIONS OF CRANMER'S BIBLE, 1540 AND 1541, PRINTED BY
GRAFTON AND WHITCHURCH: ALSO OF THE EDITIONS, IN LARGE
FOLIO, OF THE AUTHORIZED VERSION OF THE HOLY SCRIPTURES
PRINTED IN THE YEARS 1611, 1613, 1617, 1634, 1640. BY FRANCIS
FRY, F.S.A. Illustrated with Titles and with passages from the
editions, the Genealogies, and the Maps copied in fac-simile; also
with an identification of every leaf of the first seven, and of many
leaves of the other editions; on 51 Plates. Together with an
original leaf of each of the editions described. Dedicated by
permission to the Earl of Ashburnham." London: Willis &
Sotheran, Strand. Bristol: Lasbury.

"I have with great labour compared every leaf of 113 copies
of the Bibles of 1539, 1540, and 1541. Of these I found 31 to
be correct so far as they were perfect. I also examined 33
which I was not able to compare all through, and of these 32
were mixed. Thus, of 146 compared and examined, 114 proved to
be copies of mixed editions, and 31 only proved to be correct.

"The only plan that suggested itself, by which I could obtain
conclusive evidence on the differences existing in the First Edition
of the Authorised Version, was to compare the same leaf in many
copies at the same time. I have in this way compared 100 copies
of the 4 editions of the Large Folios, and examined 10 more.
Of these 70 were of the edition of 1611: 40 consisted of both
the Issues, 23 were the 1st Issue correct, 7 were the 2nd Issue
and Reprints; whilst 18 copies contained portions of subsequent
editions in the preliminary leaves or text." Of 30 copies of 1617,
1634, and 1640, 21 copies consisted of different editions mixed.
pp. 21, 22 23. Nearly all the copies both of the 1539 and the
Cranmer's and the Authorized Version were imperfect.

Whitchurch, 1553,—both inserted apparently very long since. This mixing of editions is of common occurrence; I could name many more instances.

From the facts brought forward it is certain that there was some introductory matter as well as the title printed in the same type as the text, and probable that the first part of the List of the Books occurs only on the reverse of the title; that the Bible was issued in England in 1535 with a title bearing that date printed in the English black-letter, and blank on the reverse, the introductory matter being in the same type with a List of the Books on the seventh leaf. It has also been shown that the leaf of the Dedication with "Queen Jane" is that of the edition by Nycolson, 1537, and that all the known copies of the Dedication to Henry VIII., which are of the edition of 1535, and those in the copies of 1536 read, "Queen Anne," therefore we may consider that there is not the least ground for supposing as Lewis, Professor Walter, and Anderson have done, that the publication of the First Bible in English was retarded until the year 1536, in order that the first leaf of the Dedication to the King might be re-printed with the name of Queen Jane.

If these views are correct the copy of the Sacred Scriptures, in the Library at Castle Ashby is of the

highest interest, since it must be regarded as the only
example that is known to us of the First Bible in
the English Language, surviving (except the map)
exactly in the state in which it was issued in
this country, and in the same year in which the
printing of the text was finished.

I have thus endeavoured as clearly as possible to
explain the facts which have come to my knowledge,
and if I have been able to clear up the doubts which
have hitherto existed relating to the titles and the
year of the publication of the Bible translated by
Myles Coverdale, I shall be amply rewarded for the
time I have spent in the interesting investigation.

I take this opportunity to give a short notice of
the Water-marks in the paper of the Bible 1535,
having examined every leaf of 11 Copies for the
purpose. I find a Crown, a Bull's Head, a Bull's
Head and Serpent, and seven other marks which
are figured in Plates 9, 10, 11, 12, No. 1 to 10.
As only one leaf with the mark No. 2, has occured
in these copies, it is not improbable that there may
be other water-marks in copies which I have not
examined.

The knowledge of these water-marks may be of
little value, but as facts are sometimes useful, it
is well to record them, and they may possibly assist

in deciding who was the printer. As there are in
the 11 copies, only thirty-seven examples of No. 1,
one of No. 2, and four of No. 3, the Bibles in
which most of them occur may be cited.

Sion College .... The Crown No. 1, in the New
Testament title, and in the
following leaf.
The Bull's Head and Serpent,
No. 3, in the last leaf of
Deuteronomy, folio 90.

British Museum .... Grenvelle Copy, no example
of either No. 1, 2, or 3.

British Museum .... Second Copy, the Bull's Head
and Serpent, in folio 85,
Deuteronomy, and the
Crown on the title to the
"seconde parte."

Bodleian Library .... The Crown in the title to
the "seconde parte."

Francis Fry's.... .... The Bull's Head and Serpent,
in the last leaf of Deuter-
onomy, folio 90.

Baptist College,
Bristol .... The Crown in seventeen leaves.

One Copy .... The Bull's Head and Serpent,
folio 85, Deuteronomy.

E

Glos'ter Cathedral.... The Crown in five leaves.

One Copy   ...   . The Crown in the New Testa-
                             ment title.

One Copy   .... The Bull's Head, No. 2, in
                             folio 14, Esay; the only one
                             of this mark I have seen.

One Copy   ...   . The Crown in the New Testa-
                             ment title, and in eight
                             other leaves.

No. 7 differs in shape considerably from the other
water-marks; the number in each of the 11 copies
varies from 20 to 50. There are many of the other
six shapes in all the Bibles, but they cannot always
be distinguished. Nos. 4, 5, 6, are much alike;
the number of these in each copy varies from 80 to
170. Nos. 8, 9, 10, are somewhat alike, and the
number of these varies in the same way from about
24 to 102. The water-mark No. 5 in Coverdale's
Bible is very nearly of the same form as the large
one in Tyndale's First New Testament and that in
Schœffer's Bible in German, 1529. These are figured
in my Introduction to "The First New Testament
in English. (1525 or 26,) Reproduced in fac-simile
1862," page 25: and are more like No. 5, than
Nos. 4, 6, and 8 in Coverdale, are to No. 5, though
in design the same.

I have said that it yet remains a mystery where, and by whom, this Bible was printed. It has been taken for granted by many if not by all writers on this subject, that the volume was printed on the Continent, probably judging from the type, and from the fact that the preliminary matter was printed with such type as was commonly used in England. But I believe even this much is not known. Lewis, in his History, folio edition, p. 23, says "The late *Humphrey Wanly* thought by the Types, that it was printed at *Zurich*, in the Printing-House of *Christopher Froschover.*" And this opinion appears to have been followed by most bibliographers to the present day. Including Wanly and Lewis, I have a list of fourteen writers who say that it is probable that this Bible was printed either in Zurich, Frankfort, Cologne, or Paris. The list includes Dibdin, Pearson Editor of "Remains of Coverdale," Anderson, and Lowndes.

Botfield, before quoted, says it is "supposed to have been printed in the house of *Christopher Froschover*, at Zurich; but more probably by Christian Egenolph, at Frankfort." * We are not favored with the grounds on which it was "more probably"

* "Miscellanies of the Philobiblion Society, vol. 2, article 3, London, 1855," p. 3.

E2

printed at Frankfort, which place is not again alluded to, but (p. 25) the writer quotes Wanly's opinion that the volume was printed at Zurich, and devotes several pages to the praise of Froschover and his printing.

These opinions, however, are only suppositions on a subject where evidence should be adduced. How is it that not one of the fourteen writers alluded to, has cited a work or even a line printed by Froschover, with type like any in Coverdale's Bible.

It occurred to me that as Froschover printed many works from 1522 to 1586 (see Mattaire) that if he had printed the Bible in English in 1535, he probably used the same type in other works. With the view to obtain evidence on the subject, I have examined 53 works printed by him, 41 of these in the British Museum Library, and 12 of my own, both before and after the year 1535. Many of the books are chiefly in Roman type. I find some type used in the following books the same as the two larger sizes of letters that are used in Coverdale's Bible. In the title pages of the Bible in German, 5 vols., 1527—9; in the Title of the Latin and Swiss New Testament, 1535, 4to., and in the New Testament in English, 1550, all printed by Froschover, Zurich. This is all the type I have found of this printer, like that in Coverdale's Bible.

The two sizes of type alluded to are seen in the second and third lines in the title " The Bible that, is the holy Scripture of the " [see Plate No. 1] and in the first and second lines of the first folio of Genesis, [see Plate 14, No. 1] also in the second and third titles, and at the beginning of the several books in Coverdale's Bible.

I have examined the works printed by Froschover for the water-marks; some of them have none in them, in the others are several varieties, but none of them are in the least like those in Coverdale's Bible.

The most important rival to Froschover for the honor of having been the printer of the First Bible in English is Christian Egenolph. His claim is chiefly derived, I presume, from the fact that he printed Illustrations of Scripture subjects with the monogram of Hans Sebald Beham, of Nuremberg, some of which are the same size and design as those in Coverdale's Bible. This has no doubt led to the current opinion that the wood-cuts in the Bible are by Beham, and that as Egenolph printed these illustrations therefore he printed the Bible.

Dibdin in the Decameron (vol. i. p. 169) describing the woodcuts in this Bible, says, "They are the

spirited productions of my favorite *Hans Sebald
Beham*, and have his monogram or mark expressly
introduced.   Probably they first appeared in a thin
quarto volume, published in the German language,
at Frankfort, without date." "Biblicæ Historiæ," &c.
"Egenolphus excudebat." As there is no monogram
in the wood-cuts in the Bible of 1535, I conclude
that Beham's mark alluded to, must be that on the
title-page of the work printed by Egenolph.

We find the opinions given by Dibdin followed by
other writers.   In "Memorials of Myles Coverdale,
1838," London, 8vo, the author says, (p. 24,) "It is
generally supposed, from a resemblance of the type
to that used in the printing-house of" " Froschover
at Zurich, to have been printed there." But in a
" Note," page 185 is as follows, "An eminent living
bookseller, however, is of opinion that this Bible
was printed at Franckfort, most probably by Christian
Egenolph.   This opinion he founds upon the fact,
that the identical wood-cuts, which are to be seen in
Coverdale's Bible, occur amongst others in two books
he has of that printer.   The first of these work bears
the date of 1533, the other of 1539; the one being
thus two years before the date of Coverdale's translation, the other just four years after.   Thence
follows the presumption, that if these same wood-

cuts were used at Franckfort, in 1533, and again in
1539, that they were also there in the intermediate
years. And this view, namely, that Coverdale's
Bible was printed at Franckfort, is strengthened by
the resemblance that exists between the type used in
the first of these books, and that in Coverdale's
Bible. Through the kindness of the gentleman
above alluded to, the titles of these works are here
given verbatim. The first is: "Biblisch historien,
Figurlich furgebildet, Durch den wolberumpten Sebald Behem von Nuremberg." The artist's device
ISB This in a wood-cut border. Beneath "Zu
Franckfurt, am Meyn, Bei Christian Egenolph."
At the end, the date "MDXXXIIJ." The other
is: "Biblicæ historiæ, magno artificio depictæ, &
utilitatis publicæ causa latinis Epigrammatibus a
Georgio Æmilio illustratæ." The same artist's de-
vice. In the same wood-cut border. Beneath, "Cum
Cæs. Maiestatis priuilegio, Francoforti Christianus
Egenolphus excudebat." At the end, the date,
"MDXXXIX." He has also another book of the
same printer, in which some of the wood-cuts used
in Coverdale's Bible, occur, of the date 1551.
It is entitled, "Biblia veteris Testamenti," &c.
Whether or not the foregoing proofs are sufficient
to set at rest the question of where Coverdale's

Bible was printed, it must be left to the reader to decide."

The three works named in this note are in the British Museum, but one of them is of a different year. I have examined all the wood-cuts in these books which correspond to those in Coverdale's Bible, and I can confidently state that there is not one the same. Mr. Reid the Keeper of the Prints and Drawings in the British Museum examined them with me. He allows me to give his opinion, fully supporting this statement, and to say that the difference between the wood-cuts in the books bearing Beham's monogram and the English Bible is so decided that it can be seen at a glance. Brulliot says, Hans Sebald Beham was an excellent engraver —the execution of the wood-cuts bearing his name shows the hand of a master, and are very superior to those in the Bible by Coverdale, which look like close copies. Egenolph printed some editions of the Bible in German, with illustrations. The type used in them is supposed also to prove that Egenolph printed the Bible of 1535. I have part of one of these Bibles without date. The wood-cuts in this Bible are the same as those in the books bearing Beham's monogram. If the wood-cuts used by Egenolph had been the same as Coverdale's it would not have been correct that they were in Frankfort from the year 1533 to 1539, because they were used by Nycolson, in Southwark, in 1537. The same type as the two larger sizes of type in Coverdale's Bible appears to have been used in the Bible by Egenolph, but not the type of the pages—though it is very much alike and might be taken to be the same. But if the type of two pages under comparison be not spaced out between the lines, it follows of course, that if the type is the same, the lines will range, because the body of the type is the same. But the lines are not spaced out and they do not range. Fifty three lines of Coverdale's Bible occupy the same space as fifty-four lines of Egenolph's Bible. Therefore the type cannot be the same, because the body of the type is a different size.

The following books, in addition to those by Froschover, deserve notice as containing types or wood-cuts the same as are in the Bible of 1535; the letters appear to be identical; but it must be observed, that as we cannot decide on the body of the type in single lines, there can be little doubt that if they are not identical they were struck from the same punches.

"EXOMOLOGESIS SIVE MODUS CONFITENDI," &c., 8vo, printed by Froben, Balse, 1524.

F

In this book is the same P as occurs First Epistle
of Peter, folio 95. It is drawn, Plate 13, No. 6.
When Froben used this capital it was in a good
state, but it appears to have been much worn before
it was used for the Bible, 1535.

"COMMENTARIORUM IN APOCALYPIUM IOHANNIS,"
1526, printed by Frans Birckman.

"CANTICA CANTICORUM," 1532,—

"DE DIVINIS OFFICIIS," 1532, both printed by
Arnold Birckman, Cologne, folio.

The last three works are by "Ruperti Abbatis," in
them are A, F, I, P, T, the eight-line capitals, and
A, four-line capital, the same as we find in Coverdale's Bible. These are drawn, Plate 13, Nos. 1, 2,
3, 4, 5, 7.

"The Seconde Parte" of "WM. TURNER'S HERB-
ALL," printed by Arnold Birckman, Cologne, 1562,
folio. In printing this book some type was used
the same as the large type of the Bible, 1535.

THE BIBLE BY COVERDALE, NYCOLSON, fol., 1537.

It appears probable, as has been shown, that
Nycolson printed the titles 1535 and 1536; and it
is an important fact that he has used in his edition
all the wood-cuts and side ornaments of all the titles,
and all the same wood-cuts (except two) which are
placed in the text, including those of the six "dayes

worke " on the first page of Genesis, and the wood-
cut of the tabernacle, and that of Aaron, which are
in the Bible of 1535: they are undoubtedly the same
wood-cuts. The word "LORDE" in roman appears
to be from the same type in both Bibles. There
is only one wood-cut, that of Jonah, in the folio
Bible of 1537, which is not found in that of 1535.

I have TWO NEW TESTAMENTS OF COVERDALE'S
VERSION, small 8vo.

Different editions, but much alike, without name
or date, imperfect; the wood-cuts in these are the
same as those in the Bible of 1535. These New
Testaments were printed, I have no doubt, by Nycolson, because the capitals, and the type, and the space
occupied by the words are the same as the Quarto
Bible, by Nycolson, 1537, and the lines range
with it.

THE BIBLE, 1537, QUARTO, by NYCOLSON.

There are in this the same wood-cuts of Aaron
and the tabernacle as are in the Bible, 1535.

THE BIBLE IN GERMAN, printed by PETER SCHOEF-
FER, Worms, folio 1529.

In the Bible, 1535, Esay, folio 2. is this line
" This is the prophecy of:" see Pl. 14. No. 3 no
other example of the type of this line appears in the
volume, but it is often used in Schoeffer's Bible, and

in the first New Testament in English, by W. Tyndale, which was no doubt also printed by Peter Schœffer. Type like that of this line was used by other printers.

THE GERMAN BIBLE, by DIETENBERGER, printed by Peter Jordan, Mayence, folio, 1534.

The large type is found in this book.

"THE BYBLE IN ENGLYSHE," printed by PETYT and REDMAN, for Thomas Berthelet, 1540, has the first and the New Testament titles printed from the same blocks as Coverdale's Bible.

THE BIBLE printed by DAYE and SERES, 1549.

In the titles and in the text are 49 impressions from the identical wood-cuts used for the Bible, 1535. I examined stroke with stroke, and counted the lines in a piece of shading, when comparing impressions of wood-cuts.

IN THE BIBLE printed by RAYNALDE and HYLL, 1549, and in the edition by NICOLAS HYLL, 1551, the first and the New Testament titles are from the same blocks as those in the Bible by Coverdale, when used by Nycolson.

I have examined the work entitled "CATECHISMUS EXCELSIAE Lere unde Handelinge des hilligen Christendoms," &c. "Datum Wulffenbuttel am Sontage Trinitatis Anno 1559." The two larger types of Coverdale's Bible are used in it. The type of the pages is very much like that of Coverdale, but it is not the same, the lines do not range. The printer of this book, so far as I am aware, is not known.

THE DUTCH BIBLE, printed by LIESVELT, Antwerp, 1542.

The capitals used at the beginning of the chapters in the Bible, 1535, are the same as those used in some parts of this Bible.

RICHARD JUGGE used the same wood-cuts of the four Evangelists in THE NEW TESTAMENTS of 1552 and 1553, and the large map in the BISHOP'S BIBLE, 1574, as were used in the Bible, 1535.

The large type used in the Bible by Coverdale is found in the folio BIBLE IN GERMAN, printed by HANS LUFFT, Wittemberg, 1556.

It would be gratifying to find a work by a known printer, the pages of which are the same as the pages of the First Bible in English, and having the same capitals and wood-cuts. We should like such proof as I have given* that Peter Schœffer, of Worms, printed the first New Testament in English. In works by Peter Schœffer are found all the types,

---

* See fac-similes in the Introduction to "The First New Testament printed in the English language (Worms 1525 or 1526,) translated from the Greek by William Tyndale, Reproduced in fac-simile, with an Introduction by Francis Fry, F.S.A., Bristol, printed for the Editor 1862."

the lines ranging, the wood-cut of St. Paul, the size
of the page, the numerals, and a water-mark the
same as in the New Testament.

A more extensive search than has yet been made
among the works which have issued from the Press
of Germany may bring to light similar evidence, but
I think the investigation here recorded shows that
no reliance can be placed on any of the opinions
hitherto advanced; and that we must obtain more
information before we can arrive at a satisfactory
conclusion.

Probably a fac-simile of a whole page of Coverdale's Bible has never been published; I have,
therefore, given the commencement of the Gospel of
Mark. [Plate 15.] The fourteen-line capital which
commences Genesis is drawn. [Plate 14, No. 2.]

FINIS.

Since the foregoing was printed I have obtained a copy of the work entitled
" CHRONICA/ BESCHREIBUNG vnd gemeyne anzeyge/ Bonn aller Welt herkommen/ furnamen launden/ Stande/ Engenschafften/ Historien/ wesen/ manier/ sitten/ an vnd abgang." &c. " Getruckt zu Franckenfort/ am Meyn/ Bei Christian Egenolffen." At the foot of the last page we have the date " M. D. XXXV. In Augustmon."

It is a small folio in sixes, with numerous woodcuts, about forty-three of which, some being repeated, are Scripture subjects such as we find in the Bible by Coverdale. A full page is generally fifty-two lines. This work being a small folio, dated only two months before the Bible in English 1535, we might expect the type of the pages and the woodcuts to be the same as the Bible, if Egenolph had printed the Bible. On careful examination I find that the type of the Chronicle and Egenolph's Bible in German, before alluded to, range line for line, and that both the type and wood-cuts appear identical, therefore the type of the pages and the woodcuts of the Chronicle are not the same as occur in the Bible by Coverdale. Some of the larger type in the Chronicle appear to be the same as those in Egenolph's Bible and in Coverdale's Bible.

JOHN BELLOWS, STEAM PRESS, GLOUCESTER.

Cotham Tower.

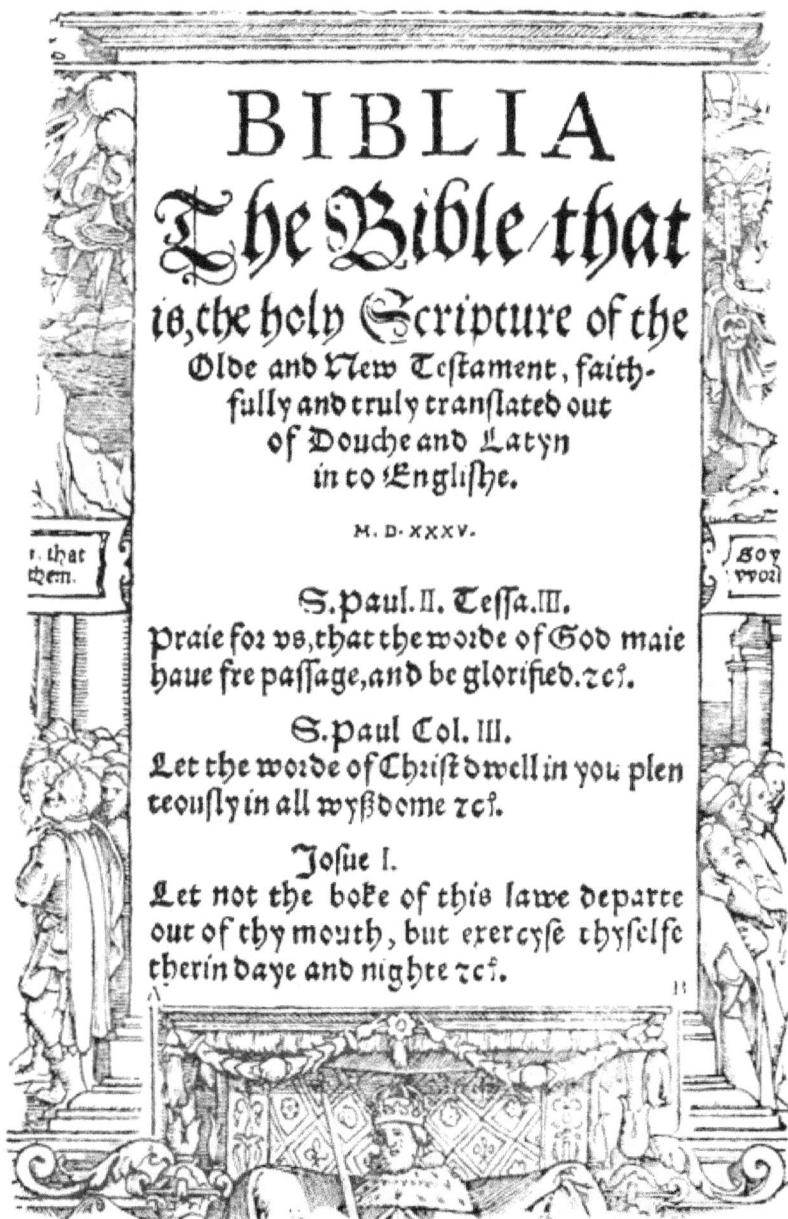

BIBLIA

The Bible/that

is, the holy Scripture of the Olde and New Testament, faithfully and truly tranſlated out of Douche and Latyn in to Engliſhe.

M. D. XXXV.

S. paul. II. Teſſa. III.
praie for vs, that the worde of God maie haue fre paſſage, and be glorified. zcʔ.

S. paul Col. III.
Let the worde of Chriſt dwell in you plenteouſly in all wyſſdome zcʔ.

Joſue I.
Let not the boke of this lawe departe out of thy mouth, but exercyſe thyſelfe therin daye and nighte zcʔ.

On the reverse of this title is
"The bokes of the whole Byble,"

BIBLIA

The Byble: that

is the holy Scrypture of the
Olde and New Testament,
faythfully translated in
to Englyshe.

M. D. XXXV.

S. Paul. II. Tessal. III.
Praye for vs, that the worde of God
maye haue fre passage & be glorified.

S. Paul. Colloss. III.
Let the worde of Christe dwell in you
plenteously in all wysdome. &c.

Josue. I.
Let not the Boke of this lawe departe
out of thy mouth, but exercyse thy selfe
therin daye and nyghte, ý thou mayest
kepe and do euery thynge accordynge
to it that is wrytten therin.

BIBLIA

The Byble: that

is/ the holy Scrypture of the
Olde and New Testament,
faythfully tranflated in
to Englyſhe.

M . D . XXXVI.

S. Paul. II. Teſſal. III.
Praye for vs, that the worde of God
maye haue fre paſſage & be gloꝛified.

S. Paul. Colloſſ. III.
Let the worde of Chꝛiſte dwell in you
plenteouſly in all wyſdome. &c.

Joſue. I.
Let not the Boke of this lawe departe
out of thy mouth, but exercyfe thy felfe
therindaye and nyghte, ꝑ thou mayeſt
kepe and do euery thynge accoꝛdynge
to it that is wꝛytten therin.

Plate 4.

THE CENTRE OF THE TITLE
NYCOLSON 1537.

ᷓ BIBLIA ᷓ
The Byble, that
is the holy Scrypture of the
Olde and New Testament, fayth=
fully translated in Englysh, and
newly ouersene & corrected.

M.D.XXXVII.

S.Paul.II.Tessa.III.

Praye for vs, that the worde of God waye haue fre
passage and be glorified.

S.Paul.II.Colloss.III.

Let the worde of Christ dwell in you plenteously in all
wysedome.

Josue.I.

Let not the Boke of this lawe departe out of thy
mouth, but exercyse thy selfe therin daye and nyght,
that thou mayest kepe and do euery thynge accordyng
to it that is wrytten therin.

⸿Imprynted in Sowthwarke for
James Nycolson.

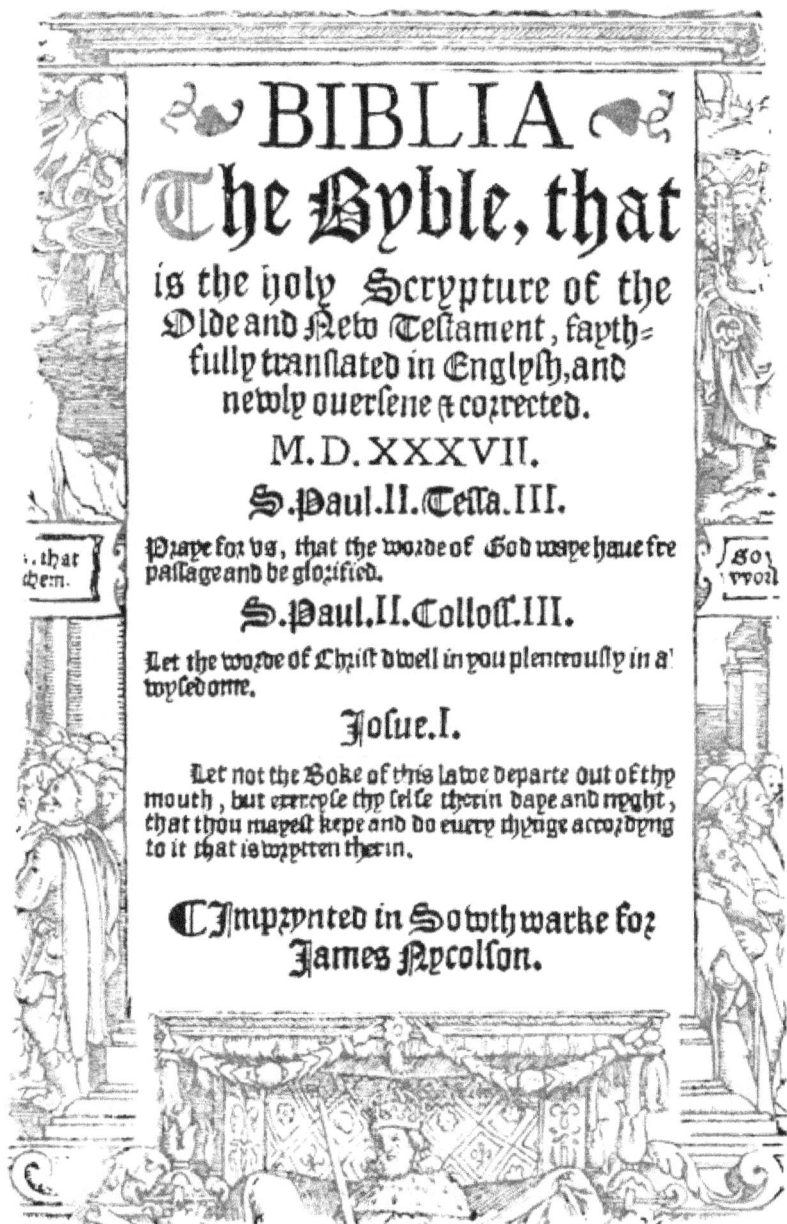

| .. that | | so |
| them. | | wod |

Unto the most victorious Prynce

Nº 1.

and oure most gracyous soueraigne Lorde, kynge Henry the eyght,
kynge of Englonde and of Fraunce, lorde of Jrlonde, &c
Defendour of the fayth, and vnder God
the chefe and supreme
heade of the
Church of Englonde.

¶ The ryght & iust administracyon of the lawes that God gaue vnto Moses
and vnto Josua: the testimonye of faythfulnes that God gaue of Dauid: the lucky
plenteous abundaunce of wysdome that God gaue vnto Salomon: the lucky
and prosperous age with the multiplicacyon of sede whiche God gaue vnto
Abraham and Sara his wyfe, begenn vnto yournost gracyous prynce, with
your dearest iust wyfe, and most bertuous Prynces, Quene Anne, Amen.

LAST LINE OF THE ABOVE LEAF & THE SIGNATURE.

Nº 2.

so, therefore. Caiphas iudgeth it to be a good dede to put Christ vnto death, that the

*.ii.

HEAD LINES &c.   THE BIBLE 1535.

Plate 6.

Nº 1.

An Epistle   **vnto the Kynges hyghnesse.**

Reverse ✠ .iiii.   ✠ b.   Nº 4.

A prologe.   Nº 3.

Myles Couerdale vnto the Christen reader.   **To the reader.**

FROM THE LEAF OF PRELIMINARY IN THE EARL OF LEICESTER'S COPY.

To the reader.

Nº 5.

are able to make satisfaction vnto God for their awne synnes: fro the whiche erroure God of his mercy preserue all his.

Now to conclude: for so moch as all the scripture is wrytten for thy doctryne and ensample, it shalbe necessary for the, to take holde vpon it, whyle it is offred the, yea and to ten handes than ffully to receaue it. And though it be not worthely magnified vnto the in this transslacion (by reason of my rudenes) yet yf thou be feruent in thy prayer, God shall

Unto the most victorious Prynce

and our most gracyous soueraygne Lorde, kynge Henry the eyght,
kynge of Englande and of Fraunce, lorde of Jrlande. &c.
Defendour of the Fayth, and vnder God
the chefe and supryme
heade of the
Church of Englande.

No. 1.

¶ The ryght & iust administracyon of the lawes that God gaue vnto Moses
and vnto Josua : the testimonye of faythfulnes that God gaue of Dauid : the
plenteous abundaunce of wysdome that God gaue vnto Salomon: the lucky
and prosperous age with the multiplicacyon of sede which God gaue vnto A=
braham and Sara his wyfe, be geuen vnto you most gracyous Prynce, with
your dearest iust wyfe, and most vertuous Pryncesse, Quene Jane, Amen.

LAST LINE OF THE ABOVE LEAF & THE SIGNATURE.

for heretye. Caiphas iudgeth it to be a good dede to put CHRIST to death, that he
✱ ✱, ii.

No. 2.

Reverse ✷✷. ii.   Nº 1.

An epiſtle.

✷ ✷ iii.   Nº 2.

Unto the kynges hyghneſſe.

7th Line.   Nº 3.

nous a trauoure to God and man

Reverse ✷✷. iiii.   Nº 4.

A prologe.

✷ ✷ v.   Nº 5.

To the reader.

Myles Couerdale vnto the Chriſten reader.

Nº 6.

Youre graces humble ſub=
iecte and daylye oratour,
Myles Couerdale.
✷ ✷ iiii.

The Conclusion.   Youre graces humble ſub=
Dedⁿ to the king.   iecte and daylye oratour,
Nycolson. 1537.   Myles Couerdale.

The Conclusion.   Youre graces humble ſub=   Nº 7.
Dedⁿ to the king.   iecte and daylye oratour,
1535.   Myles Couerdale.
✷ iiii.

Plate 9.

THE BIBLE, 1535.
WATER MARKS.

Nº 1.

Nº 3.

Nº 2.

Plate 10.

THE BIBLE, 1535.
WATER MARKS.

Nº 4.

Nº 5.

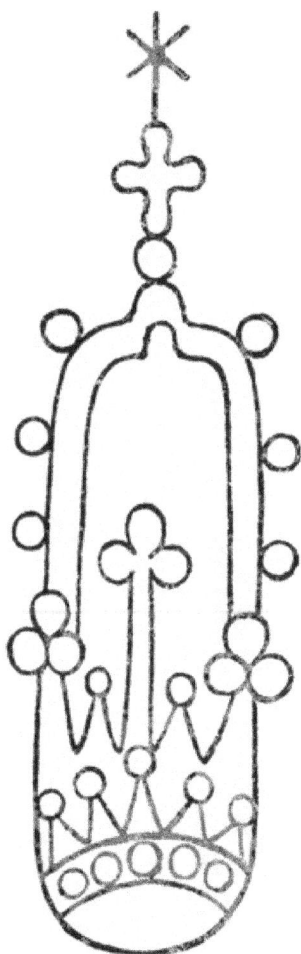

THE BIBLE, 1535.
WATER MARKS.

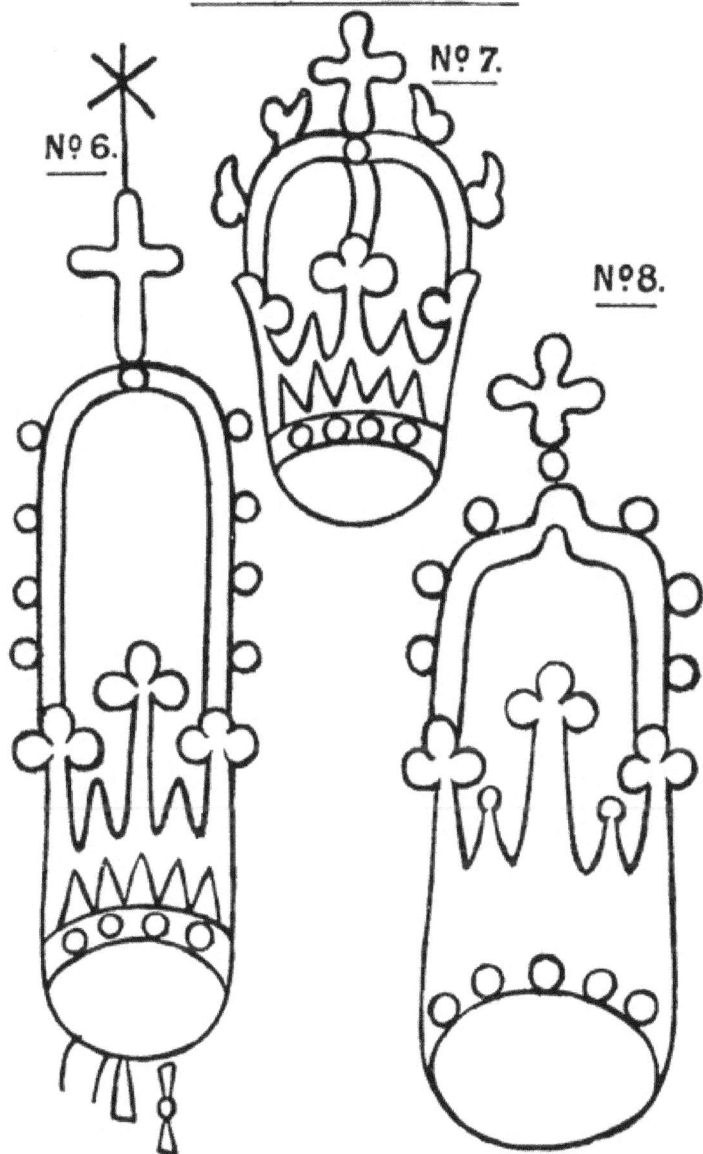

Plate II.

Nº 7.

Nº 6.

Nº 8.

Plate 12.

THE BIBLE, 1535.
WATER MARKS.

No 9.

No 10.

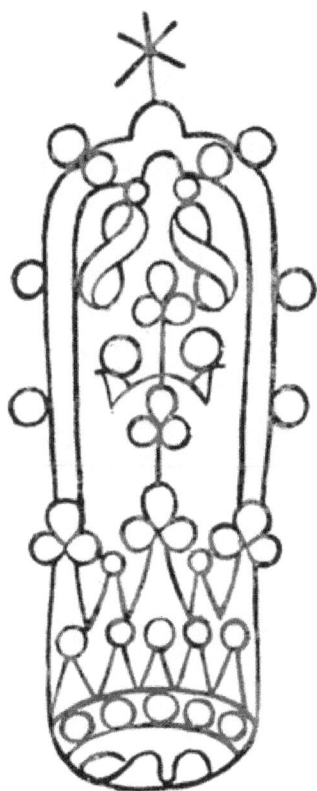

Plate 13.

SOME OF THE CAPITALS USED IN
THE BIBLE IN FOLIO 1535.

Nº 1.

Nº 2.

Nº 3.

Nº 4.

Nº 5.

Nº 6.

Nº 7.

The first boke of Mo=
ſes, called Genesis.

The firſt Chapter.

A
4.Eſd.6.d
Eccli.18.a
Iere.10.b
Heb.11.a
Eſa.44.c

Nº 2.

IN ẏ begyn
nynge God
created hea
uen ʒ earth:
and ẏ earth
was voyde
and emptie,
and darck-
nes was v-
pon the de-
pe,ʒ ẏ ſpre-
te of God
moued vpõ
the water.
And God ſayde: let there be light,ʒ there
was light. And God ſawe the light that it
was good. Then God deuyded ẏ light from

Nº 3. *Eſay, Folio 2.*

This is the prophecy of

Nº 4. *Imprint, Last Page.*

Prynted in the yeare of oure LORDE M. D. XXXV.
and fyniſhed the fourth daye of October.

Luce 3.
Johan. d

Some
reade:

*Jn whom
J delyte.
Jam pa
cified.

Mat.4.a
Luc.4.a

Jesus came out of Galile from Nazareth, and was baptysed of Jhon in Jordan. And as soone as he was come out of the water, he sawe that the heauens opened, and the goost as a doue comynge downe vpon him. And there came a voyce from heaue: Thou art my deare sonne, *in whom J delyte.

And immediatly the sprete droue him in to the wyldernes: and he was in the wylder nes fourtye dayes, and was tempted of Sa

Mat.8.b

Luc.4.c

and Andrew, th James and Jhon. And Sy- mons mother in lawe laye: had the feuers, and anone they tolde him of her. And he ca me to her, and set her vp, and toke her by þ hande, and the feuer left her immediatly. And þei mynistred vnto them.

At euen whan the Sonne was gone downe, they brought vnto him all that we- re sick and possessed, and the whole cite was gathered together at the dore, and

CC iiij

An exact copy of a page of the Bible
by Coverdale 1535.   Plate 15.

The gospell

of S. Marke. Fo. xvi.

Jesus came out of Galile from Nazareth, and was baptysed of Jhon in Jordan. And as soone as he was come out of the water, he sawe that the heauens opened, and the goost as a doue commynge downe vpon him. And there came a voyce from heaue: Thou art my deare sonne, in whom I delyte.

And immediatly the sprete droue him in to the wyldernes: and he was in the wylder nes fourtye dayes, and was tempted of Sa

and Andrew, wt James and Jhon. And Symons mother in lawe laye sicke of the feuers, and anone they tolde him of her. And he came to her, and set her vp, and toke her by y hande, and the feuer left her immediatly. And she mynistred vnto them.

At euen whan the Sonne was gone downe, they brought vnto him all that were sicke and possessed, and the whole cite was gathered together at the dore, and

C C iiij

An exact copy of a page of the Bible
by Coverdale 1535.   Plate 15.

THE FIRST NEW TESTAMENT

PRINTED IN THE ENGLISH LANGUAGE,

(WORMS, 1525 or 1526.)

TRANSLATED BY WILLIAM TYNDALE:

REPRODUCED IN FAC-SIMILE,

WITH AN INTRODUCTION

BY FRANCIS FRY, F. S. A.

BRISTOL: PRINTED FOR THE EDITOR—1862.

William Tyndale having completed his translation of the New Testament from the Greek, went to Cologne, intending there to print it. Not being successful he removed to Worms,

ERRATA.

Page 6, line 20, for *Dibden* read *Dibdin*.

„ 17 „ 7 „ *Lord Compton,* read *Lord A. Compton*.

„ 25 „ 11 „ *Grenzelle,* read *Grenville*.

„ 27 note „ *Philobiblion,* read *Philobiblon*.

„ 30 „ 22 „ *work,* read *works*.

I have devoted so much time to this careful examination, in order that the accuracy of the work may be relied on.

The paper, on which this New Testament is printed has been expressly manufactured to imitate the colour and appearance of the original. It is *hand-made*, the fine and cross wires being placed in the paper maker's mould so as to produce the same wire marks as appear in the paper used by Schoeffer. The large paper copies are printed on the same paper, only thicker.

The whole impression consists of 177 copies, of which 26 are in quarto. To produce these, the entire text has been transferred from the 88 stones used in printing the octavo size, to 176 stones

**Fold
Out**

THE FIRST NEW TESTAMENT

PRINTED IN THE ENGLISH LANGUAGE,

(WORMS, 1525 or 1526,)

TRANSLATED BY WILLIAM TYNDALE:

REPRODUCED IN FAC-SIMILE,

WITH AN INTRODUCTION

BY FRANCIS FRY, F. S. A.

BRISTOL: PRINTED FOR THE EDITOR—1862.

William Tyndale having completed his translation of the
New Testament from the Greek, went to Cologne, intending
there to print it. Not being successful he removed to Worms,

ERRATA.

Page 6, line 20, for *Dibden* read *Dibdin*.

„ 17 „ 7 „ *Lord Compton*, read *Lord A.
Compton.*

„ 25 „ 11 „ *Grenvelle.* read *Grenville.*

„ 27 note „ *Philobiblion*, read *Philobiblon*.

„ 30 „ 22 „ *work*, read *works*.

I have devoted so much time to this careful examination, in
order that the accuracy of the work may be relied on.

The paper, on which this New Testament is printed has been
expressly manufactured to imitate the colour and appearance of
the original. It is *hand-made*, the fine and cross wires being
placed in the paper maker's mould so as to produce the same
wire marks as appear in the paper used by Schœffer. The large
paper copies are printed on the same paper, only thicker.

The whole impression consists of 177 copies, of which 26 are
in quarto. To produce these, the entire text has been transferred
from the 88 stones used in printing the octavo size, to 176 stones

THE FIRST NEW TESTAMENT

PRINTED IN THE ENGLISH LANGUAGE,

(WORMS, 1525 or 1526,)

TRANSLATED BY WILLIAM TYNDALE:

REPRODUCED IN FACSIMILE,

WITH AN INTRODUCTION

BY FRANCIS FRY, F.S.A.

BRISTOL: PRINTED FOR THE EDITOR—1862.

William Tyndale having completed his translation of the New Testament from the Greek, went to Cologne, intending there to print it. Not being successful he removed to Worms, where there is no doubt he accomplished the work, and gave to his countrymen the New Testament, which was the first printed in the English language.

This is a reproduction of the only known copy of the first edition of Tyndale's New Testament, perhaps the most interesting book in our language. It contains 692 pages of close small type; is a faithful representation of the original; and will be valued not only as a Version, but as shewing the state of the English language, the style of the printing, the orthography, (which is very irregular,) the punctuation, the divisions of the words at the ends of lines, (even to a letter,) and the contractions used. It has been made by tracing on transfer paper, placing this on lithographic-stones, and then printing it in the usual way: a method evidently calculated to ensure the closest possible correspondence with the original.

To prove the correctness of the work, I have compared a proof of every page, folding it so as to place each line parallel with, and close to, the same line in the original; so that, by comparing the line all along, I could easily see that it was correct. *In this way I have examined every line throughout the volume,* and I believe that not a single incorrect letter will be found in it. I have devoted so much time to this careful examination, in order that the accuracy of the work may be relied on.

The paper, on which this New Testament is printed has been expressly manufactured to imitate the colour and appearance of the original. It is *handmade*, the fine and cross wires being placed in the paper maker's mould so as to produce the same wire marks as appear in the paper used by Schoeffer. The large paper copies are printed on the same paper, only thicker.

The whole impression consists of 177 copies, of which 26 are in quarto. To produce these, the entire text has been transferred from the 88 stones used in printing the octavo size, to 176 stones required for the quarto size, so as to obtain the wider inside and top margins. The work has been effaced from the stones.

The Introduction contains a brief notice of the early life of Tyndale, and of his printing the New Testament at Worms; and the evidence that I have collected to prove that Peter Schœffer was the printer; to which are added 7 pages of fac-similes from books printed by him, and the water marks in the Testament, and Schœffer's Bible; a description and history of the only known copy, which is in the Baptist College, Bristol, with a page, the beginning of the first epistle of St. Peter, with the wood-cut of the Apostle, illuminated and ruled with red lines, like the original. Also a list of the works printed by Peter Schœffer, of Worms.

In the original, the wood-cuts, capitals, &c., 2606 in number, are illuminated; copies so illuminated, also on large paper, on old paper and on vellum, may be obtained on special application.

Octavo, Cloth, £8.

A DESCRIPTION OF THE GREAT BIBLE, 1539,
AND THE SIX EDITIONS OF
CRANMER'S BIBLE, 1540 AND 1541:
ALSO OF THE EDITIONS, IN LARGE FOLIO, OF THE AUTHORIZED VERSION OF THE HOLY SCRIPTURES PRINTED IN THE YEARS 1611, 1613, 1617, 1634, 1640.

BY FRANCIS FRY, F.S.A.

[*The full Title is given page 24*]

THIS work is intended to serve not only as a bibliographical description of the folios above-named, but also as a key whereby to identify the editions, and the evidence afforded from the comparison of a large number of copies has, it is hoped, decided some doubts relating to them. The folio size has been adopted to admit of the best arrangements of the passages to be compared, and the insertion of the ORIGINAL LEAVES.

I have for many years been collecting editions of the Bible and New Testament, especially the earlier ones; part of my plan having been to obtain a complete set of the Seven Editions, and the Large Folios of the Authorized Version named in the Title; in which I have succeeded. Of the 7 editions, five having 62 lines on a page, read together; and 2 editions having 65 lines on a page, and the same two editions with reprints, read together, while some of the preliminary leaves and internal titles will suit any edition; therefore any portion of these respectively may be bound together, the first and last word of every leaf of the 5 editions, and of the 2 editions, and the

Reprints, being the same with one or two accidental exceptions. Most copies are found to consist of these editions mixed. [See quotation p. 22.] Every leaf of the 7 differs with the exception of 14 leaves. I have found, however, but few of these Bibles which do not contain some leaves of other editions. Thus the 1539 and April 1549 editions are often found mixed, so also the July and December, and the 2 editions and the Reprints having 65 lines.

The folio editions of our Authorized Version of 1611, 1617, 1634, and 1640, and the preliminary of 1613, also have the first and last word of the same leaf in each edition the same, excepting 2 pages in 1634, and are printed with the same type, and on a page of the same size, but differently set up. These all read together, and copies are often found composed of parts of two or more editions. From the facts elicited I think it conclusively shown which is the first and which is the second issue.

By this work every leaf of the Great Bible, and the Six Cranmers, and the Reprints, can be identified; also the Preliminary of the editions of the Authorized Version described, and one leaf in every signature of both Issues 1611, the Reprints, the 1617, and the 1634. A collation and full description of each of the editions, and those with Reprints is given. The edition of April 1540 is shown to be the first of Cranmer's Version. The two titles belonging to the edition of 1611 are described, and full consideration is given to the question, whether both were intended for the same volume, or for either issue.

The Genealogies of Jesus Christ, and the Map of Canaan, which were published with the A. V., are described. There are 23 varieties of the Genealogies in folio. There are 11 varieties of the Map. They are printed from two copper-plates, and a portion of each is copied, and a passage from each of the six editions of the letter-press on the reverse of the Map.

I have inserted an original leaf, from each of the 13 editions described, and one from the Reprints, 1611.

I have collated every leaf of 45 copies of the 2nd issue, and 41 of these differ from each other. To show how the Reprints and 1st Issue have been used in each copy of the 2nd Issue to present so remarkable a result, a Table in 45 columns is given, which shows the distribution of them through each volume.

Demy Folio, on thick toned paper, the Plates on Imitation Old Paper made expressly, £5. A few copies on fine Vellum £20.

Willis & Sotheran, London. Lasbury, Bristol.

THE PROPHETE JONAS,

WITH AN INTRODUCTION BEFORE TEACHINGE TO UNDERSTONDE HIM,
BY WILLIAM TYNDALE.
TO WHICH IS ADDED COVERDALE'S VERSION OF JONAH,
WITH AN INTRODUCTION BY FRANCIS FRY. 8vo., 1863.

Price 10s. On *Old* Paper £1. A few copies on Vellum £2 10s.

This work has been so long lost that no copy was known to exist.
Lord Arthur Hervey lately found a copy in his library bound in a
volume with other tracts. Tyndale's version has never appeared since
the original edition now copied. It is not in the first nor any other
edition of the Bible called "Tyndale's.

A PROPER DIALOGE

BETWENE A GENTILLMAN AND A HUSBANDMAN ECHE COMPLAYNYNGE TO OTHER THEIR
MISERABLE CALAMITE THROUGH THE AMBICION OF THE CLERGYE. WITH

COMPENDIOUS OLDE TREATYSE

SHEWYNGE HOWE THAT WE OUGHT TO HAVE THE SCRIPTURE IN ENGLYSSHE,
PRINTED BY HANS LUFT, 1530.
WITH AN INTRODUCTION BY FRANCIS FRY. 8vo., 1863.

Price 10s. On *Old* Paper £1. A few copies on Vellum £2 10s.

These are one book being printed on four sheets, signatures A B C D.
The author or editor is unknown. They were written by some one
who strongly advocated the *new learning*. The Dialogue is in rhyme.
The only copy of the original edition which is known, is bound in the
same volume with Tyndale's Jonah.

THE SOULDIERS POCKET BIBLE.

PRINTED AT LONDON BY G. B. AND R. W. FOR G. C. 1643.
WITH AN INTRODUCTION BY F. FRY. 8vo., 1862.

Price 5s. A few copies on Vellum £1 5s.

"Containing the most (if not all) those places contained in holy
Scripture, which doe shew the qualifications of his inner man, that is a fit
Souldier to fight the Lords Battels, both before the fight, in the fight,
and after the fight."

There has been a prevalent opinion that the Soldiers in Cromwell's
Army were supplied with a Pocket Bible, but as to what edition of the
Bible was used there has hitherto been no evidence. That this was the
Pocket Bible there can be no doubt. One copy only of this tract is
known in this Kingdom, which is in the British Museum.

THE CHRISTIAN SOLDIER'S PENNY BIBLE.

SHEWING FROM THE HOLY SCRIPTURES THE SOLDIER'S
DUTY AND ENCOURAGEMENT,
LONDON: PRINTED BY R. SMITH, FOR SAM. WADE, 1693.
WITH AN INTRODUCTORY NOTE BY F. FRY. 8vo., 1862. PRICE 5s.

This is also a rare tract. It is nearly a reprint of the Souldiers Pocket
Bible, somewhat altered.

www.ingramcontent.com/pod-product-compliance
Lightning Source LLC
Chambersburg PA
CBHW020306090426
42735CB00009B/1235